SPORTS' GREATEST OF ALL TIME

BOXING'S G.O.A.T.

MUHAMMAD ALI, MANNY PACQUIAO, AND MORE

JON M. FISHMAN

Lerner Publications ◆ Minneapolis

SCORE BIG with sports fans, reluctant readers, and report writers!

Lerner Sports is a database of high-interest biographies profiling notable sports superstars. Packed with fascinating facts, these bios explore the backgrounds, career-defining moments, and everyday lives of popular athletes. Lerner Sports is perfect for young readers developing research skills or looking for exciting sports content.

LERNER SPORTS FEATURES:

- ☑ Keyword search
- ☑ Topic navigation menus
- ☑ Fast facts
- ☑ Related bio suggestions to encourage more reading
- ☑ Admin view of reader statistics
- ☑ Fresh content updated regularly
- and more!

Visit LernerSports.com for a free trial!

Lerner **SPORTS**

Lerner Publications Company
An imprint of Lerner Publishing Group, Inc.
241 First Avenue North
Minneapolis, MN 55401 USA

For reading levels and more information, look up this title at www.lernerbooks.com.

Main body text set in Aptifer Sans LT Pro. Typeface provided by Linotype AG.

Editor: Brianna Kaiser **Designer:** Kim Morales

Library of Congress Cataloging-in-Publication Data

Names: Fishman, Jon M., author.
Title: Boxing's G.O.A.T: Muhammad Ali, Manny Pacquiao, and more / Jon M. Fishman.
Description: Minneapolis : Lerner Publications, [2022] | Series: Sports' greatest of all time (Lerner sports) | Includes bibliographical references and index. | Audience: Ages 7–11 | Audience: Grades 2–3 | Summary: "It's time to enter the ring and meet the greatest boxers of all time! Readers will learn about the sport and look at exciting facts and stats presented in an engaging top-10 format"—Provided by publisher.
Identifiers: LCCN 2020052672 (print) | LCCN 2020052673 (ebook) | ISBN 9781728428635 (library binding) | ISBN 9781728431628 (paperback) | ISBN 9781728430836 (ebook)
Subjects: LCSH: Boxers (Sports)—Rating of—Juvenile literature. | Boxers (Sports)—Biography—Juvenile literature. | Boxing—Juvenile literature. | Ali, Muhammad, 1942–2016—Juvenile literature. | Pacquiao, Manny, 1978– —Juvenile literature.
Classification: LCC GV1131 .F564 2022 (print) | LCC GV1131 (ebook) | DDC 796.83—dc23

LC record available at https://lccn.loc.gov/2020052672
LC ebook record available at https://lccn.loc.gov/2020052673

Manufactured in the United States of America
1-49400-49501-4/14/2021

TABLE OF CONTENTS

ROUND ONE

Boxing's history is jam-packed with incredible champions. But how do you choose the greatest of all time (G.O.A.T.)? Picking the best athletes is never easy. In the United States, some pro sports leagues have competed for more than 100 years.

FACTS AT A GLANCE

WILLIE PEP fought in almost 250 pro boxing matches. He lost only 11 times.

MANNY PACQUIAO has won world championships in eight different weight classes. That's more than any other boxer in history.

FLOYD MAYWEATHER JR.'S pro boxing career lasted for more than 20 years. He retired with an undefeated record.

During World War II (1939–1945), **JOE LOUIS** fought in almost 100 boxing matches to entertain US Army troops. The matches aren't included in his official boxing record.

Equipment, rules, and strategies change with time. That makes it a challenge to compare athletes from different eras.

Boxing's history is much longer than the histories of most other sports. Middle Eastern carvings from 5,000 years ago show a form of boxing. In 688 BCE, boxing became a sport at the Olympic Games in Greece. The fighters wore soft, thin strips of leather on their hands and forearms.

In Europe, boxing's popularity rose again in the 1700s. Some fighters began to wear padded gloves to protect their hands. In the 1800s, boxing matches adopted many of the rules that modern fights use. Matches took place in a square ring surrounded by ropes. Biting, headbutting, and hitting below the belt were banned. After a long break, the Olympics restarted in 1896, and boxers began competing at the Games again in 1904. In 2012, women's boxing became an official Olympic sport.

Amateur boxers compete at the Olympics and other competitions such as the Pan American Games. They gain experience to become pro fighters. The top pro boxers fight

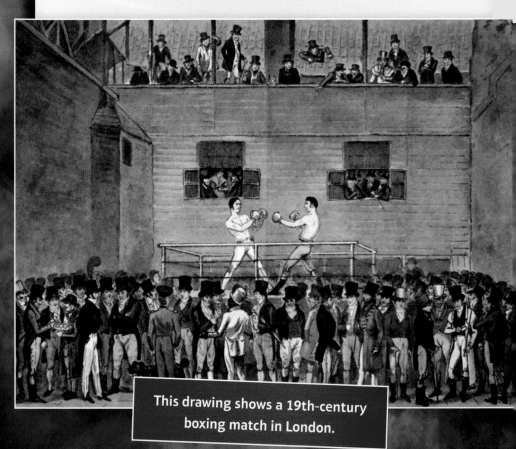

This drawing shows a 19th-century boxing match in London.

Dayana Sanchez (*left*) and Beatriz Soares Ferreira (*right*) compete at the 2019 Pan American Games in Lima, Peru.

in matches around the world and earn millions of dollars in prize money.

Boxing's long history makes it even harder to choose the G.O.A.T. As you learn more about the sport, you'll probably have your own ideas about the best fighters to step into the ring. That's fine. Learning about boxing and forming your own opinions is part of the fun!

SUGAR RAY LEONARD

Ray Charles Leonard began boxing at 14 in Landover, Maryland. He was quick and smart in the ring. And he loved to fight. Leonard won several national amateur boxing titles. In 1976, he traveled to Montreal, Canada, to compete in the Olympic Games. Despite suffering hand injuries, he won the gold medal in his weight class.

After the Olympics, Leonard became a pro fighter to earn money to help his family. He won his first pro match as a 20-year-old in 1977. He went on to beat some of the world's top boxers, including Roberto Durán, Thomas Hearns, and Marvin Hagler. Leonard won world titles in five different weight classes. No other fighter had done that at the time. He retired from the ring in 1997 and became an author and boxing broadcaster.

SUGAR RAY LEONARD STATS

- He ended his pro career with 36 wins, 3 losses, and 1 draw (36–3–1).

- Leonard won three amateur national Golden Gloves titles as the best boxer in his weight class.

- He won 25 pro fights by knockout.

- He joined the International Boxing Hall of Fame in 1997.

- His nickname, Sugar Ray Leonard, was inspired by one of his boxing heroes, Sugar Ray Robinson.

#9

WILLIE PEP

Big punches and knockouts get most of the attention from boxing fans. But defense is just as important to win a match. Some boxing experts consider Willie Pep the best defender ever. With his quick foot and head movements, he could beat an opponent by avoiding punches. Pep once won a round without landing a punch. The judges decided he controlled the action with his defense.

Pep's pro career began in 1940. He won 63 fights in a row before losing a close match to Sammy Angott in 1943. Then Pep went on a streak of 73 straight victories. He held the world title in the featherweight class from 1942 to 1948. Pep retired in 1959. In 1965, he returned to the boxing ring and won nine straight fights. He retired for good after losing to Calvin Woodland in 1966. It was just the 11th loss of Pep's long career.

WILLIE PEP STATS

- Pep finished his career with a 230–11–1 record.

- In his pro career, he won 65 fights by knockout.

- Pep beat Chalky Wright in 15 rounds to win the featherweight title in 1942.

- Pep returned to the ring in June 1947 after suffering several injuries, including a broken leg, in a plane crash five months earlier.

- He became a member of the International

JACK JOHNSON

Much of the United States was segregated when Black boxer Jack Johnson began his career in the late 1800s. White fighters refused to step into the ring with Johnson because of the color of his skin. So Johnson fought against other people of color. He developed a tough boxing style. He stayed cautious in the early rounds and studied his opponents' moves. As the fight

progressed, Johnson would become more aggressive and punch with power.

In 1908, white heavyweight champion Tommy Burns agreed to fight Johnson. Johnson knocked out Burns in the 14th round. Many white boxing fans in the United States were unhappy with Johnson's success. To try to take the title from Johnson, former white champion Jim Jeffries came out of retirement in 1910. Johnson beat Jeffries in 15 rounds. Johnson held the heavyweight title until 1915.

JACK JOHNSON STATS

▶ Johnson racked up a career record of 77–13–14.

▶ He won his first pro fight in 1897.

▶ In 1908, Johnson became the first Black heavyweight champion of the world.

▶ About 20,000 fans watched Johnson beat Tommy Burns for the title in 1908.

▶ Johnson joined the International Boxing Hall of Fame in 1990.

MANNY PACQUIAO

Manny Pacquiao grew up in the Philippines. In 1995, at 16, he fought his first pro boxing match. His high-energy style and lightning-fast punches made him a force in the ring. He won his first world title in 1998.

Pacquiao moved around to different weight classes throughout his career. In 2009, he became champion in

his seventh weight class, setting an all-time record. A year later, Pacquiao moved up in weight class to beat Antonio Margarito for another world championship. At the time of the fight, Margarito outweighed Pacquiao by 17 pounds (7.7 kg).

Known as Pac-Man to his fans, Pacquiao is one of the world's most popular athletes. He's also an actor, a musician, and a politician. He served two terms in the Philippines House of Representatives. In 2016, he won a seat in the country's Senate.

MANNY PACQUIAO STATS

- Pacquiao has a career record of 62–7–2.

- He has knocked out 39 opponents.

- Pacquiao won **championships** in eight different weight classes, an all-time record.

- He won the *Ring* magazine Fighter of the Year award three times.

- The World Boxing Council named Pacquiao the Fighter of the Decade for 2001–2010.

ROBERTO DURÁN

Roberto Durán's nickname, Hands of Stone, says it all. He punched as hard as any fighter in boxing history. In his pro career, Durán knocked out almost 60 percent of his opponents. He began fighting as a pro in 1968 and racked up 31 straight victories. After losing to Esteban de Jesus at New York's Madison Square Garden in 1972,

Durán started a 41-match winning streak.

Durán's boxing career spanned five decades, a rare feat for a top fighter. He boxed until the age of 49. Most of his losses came in his later years. On July 14, 2001, he lost to Héctor Camacho in Denver, Colorado. Durán still wasn't ready to give up fighting. But in October, he was seriously injured in a car accident. He recovered and finally retired from boxing a few months later.

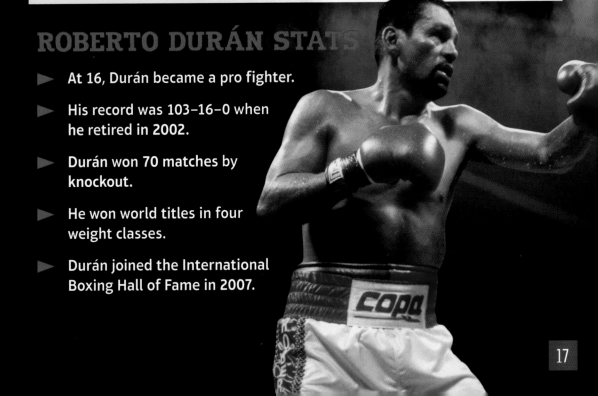

ROBERTO DURÁN STATS

▶ At 16, Durán became a pro fighter.

▶ His record was 103–16–0 when he retired in 2002.

▶ Durán won 70 matches by knockout.

▶ He won world titles in four weight classes.

▶ Durán joined the International Boxing Hall of Fame in 2007.

HENRY ARMSTRONG

In July 1931, Henry Armstrong began his pro career with a match against Al Iovino. Iovino knocked out Armstrong. A little over a year later, Armstrong's record stood at just 1–4–0. But he seemed to get better with each fight. At the beginning of 1937, his record had improved to 52–10–6. That year Armstrong fought an incredible 27 matches. He won all the fights and ended 25 of them by knockout.

In the ring, Armstrong attacked with speed and power. He threw furious, nonstop punches that overwhelmed opponents. His aggressive style earned him many nicknames, including Hurricane Henry, Hammering Henry, and Human Buzzsaw. It also made him an incredible boxing champion. Armstrong is the only fighter in boxing history to hold world titles in three weight classes at the same time.

HENRY ARMSTRONG STATS

▶ Armstrong had a 151–22–10 career record.

▶ He knocked out 101 opponents.

▶ Opponents knocked out Armstrong just two times.

▶ Armstrong retired from pro boxing in 1945.

▶ He became a member of the International Boxing Hall of Fame in 1990.

#4

FLOYD MAYWEATHER JR.

Floyd Mayweather Jr. was born to be a great boxing champion. His father and uncle were both pro fighters. As soon as Floyd could walk, he began going to the gym with his father. He received his first pair of boxing gloves when he was seven.

Floyd Mayweather Jr. might be the best defensive fighter in boxing history. His quickness and ability to predict opponents' moves helped him avoid big punches. His face was often unmarked at the end of fights, earning him the nickname Pretty Boy. In 50 career matches, he was knocked down just once. On October 11, 1996, Mayweather won his first pro match. Almost 21 years later, he retired from boxing with an undefeated record.

FLOYD MAYWEATHER JR. STATS

► Mayweather won a bronze medal at the 1996 Summer Olympics in Atlanta, Georgia.

► His pro record was a perfect 50-0-0.

► Mayweather won 27 matches by knockout.

► He won world titles in five different weight classes.

► In 2015, Mayweather beat Manny Pacquiao in a match fans called the Fight of the Century.

JOE LOUIS

When Joe Louis ruled the boxing world in the mid-20th century, many of his fellow fighters were sluggers. They tried to knock out opponents as quickly as possible with huge, powerful punches. Louis could match anyone in power. But his defense and precise style set him apart. He didn't dance around the ring. He stood toe-to-toe with opponents. Then he would unleash lightning-quick punches with both hands.

Louis's first pro fight came in 1934. He didn't lose a match until two years later. In June 1937, he beat former titleholder James Braddock to become the heavyweight champion of the world. Louis held the title until he retired in March 1949. No fighter in boxing history has held onto a world title for as long as Louis did. He returned to the ring in 1950 and won eight more fights before retiring again in 1951.

JOE LOUIS STATS

- Louis had an incredible career record of 68–3–0.

- He set a record by holding the heavyweight title for 11 years and eight months.

- He won 54 pro matches by knockout.

- Louis successfully defended the heavyweight title 25 times.

- Louis joined the US Army in 1942. To entertain his fellow troops, he fought in 96 unofficial boxing matches around the world between 1942 and 1945.

SUGAR RAY ROBINSON

In the early 1930s, coach George Gainford started a boxing club in Harlem, New York. One of the club's fighters was a young boy whose moves were so sweet that Gainford nicknamed him Sugar. As a boxer, Sugar Ray Robinson was almost perfect. His punches were fast, accurate, and packed with power. He moved around the ring with agility and balance. And he knew when to attack and when to play defense.

Robinson fought almost 90 times as an amateur and never lost. Then he won his first 40 pro matches before losing to the legendary Jake LaMotta in February 1943. Robinson wouldn't lose again until July 1951. He boxed until the age of 45, with his pro career spanning three decades. Of Robinson's 19 career losses, 10 of them came when he was 40 or older.

SUGAR RAY ROBINSON STATS

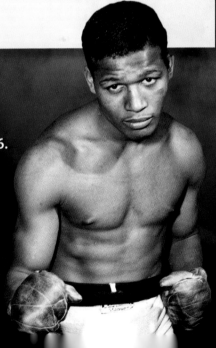

► Robinson's record was an amazing 175–19–6.

► He knocked out 109 opponents.

► He won the middleweight class world title a record five times.

► In his career, he fought 18 current or former world champions.

► He won the *Ring* magazine Fighter of the Year award in 1942 and 1951.

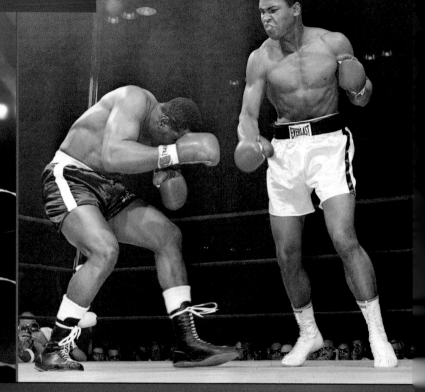

#1

MUHAMMAD ALI

Muhammad Ali's global fame was unmatched in sports history. Outside the ring, he charmed reporters and fans with his personality. Inside, he danced and ducked away from opponents as he delivered quick, mighty punches.

Ali, then known as Cassius Clay Jr., fought at the 1960 Olympics in Rome, Italy. After winning gold, he returned home to Louisville, Kentucky, and began his pro career.

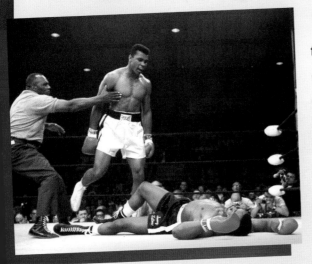

In 1964, he won the heavyweight championship and changed his name to Muhammad Ali. In the late 1960s, Ali became a hero to many by refusing to fight in the Vietnam War (1954–1975). The legal dispute kept him out of the ring for more than three years. He returned and became the first fighter to win the heavyweight title three times. Ali's dominance in the ring, impact on society, and worldwide fame make him the greatest boxer of all time.

MUHAMMAD ALI STATS

- Ali's career record was 56–5–0.

- He won 37 matches by knockout.

- He won the heavyweight title in 1964, 1974, and 1978.

- Ali fought in some of boxing's most famous matches, including his defeat of Joe Frazier at the Thrilla in Manila.

- His nickname was the Greatest.

YOUR
G.O.A.T.

BOXING'S GREATEST CHAMPIONS reached the top of their sport in different ways. Some attacked fearlessly, while others focused on defense. A few fighters attracted fans by letting their personalities shine in and out of the ring. Learn more about the boxers in this book and other fighters by checking out the Learn More section on page 31. Talk to friends and family who like boxing to see what they think. You can also ask your librarians and teachers for more boxing information.

As you learn more about some of boxing's top fighters, your opinions about some of them might change. That's great! Make your own top 10 list of boxers, and compare it to the fighters in this book. Where do you agree and disagree? When it comes to your personal top 10, it's all up to you!

BOXING FACTS

► The earliest boxing matches had no rounds and no judges. The fight went on until one of the contestants gave up or couldn't continue.

► Heavyweight boxer Mike Tyson punched with as much force as any fighter in history. He won 50 fights from 1985 to 2005, and 44 of those victories came by knockout. Tyson knocked out 22 of his opponents in the first round!

► On February 22, 2020, 273-pound (124 kg) Tyson Fury became the heavyweight champion of the world. But he wasn't the heaviest heavyweight of all time. When Russia's Nikolai Valuev won the title in 2005, he weighed a shocking 324 pounds (147 kg).

► In 1999, *Sports Illustrated* magazine named Muhammad Ali the greatest athlete of the 20th century.

GLOSSARY

agility: the ability to move quickly and easily

amateur: a person who takes part in sports for pleasure and not for pay

broadcaster: a person who talks during a sports event on TV

draw: a boxing match that ends without a winner and a loser

judge: a person who decides the winner of a boxing match. Most boxing matches have three judges.

knockout: the end of a boxing match when one boxer has been knocked down and is unable to rise and resume boxing

pro: taking part in a sport to make money

round: a unit of a boxing match. Most rounds last three minutes.

segregated: separated by race in places such as schools and hospitals

weight class: a group of boxers defined by how much the fighters weigh

LEARN MORE

Leed, Percy. *Muhammad Ali: I Am the Greatest.* Minneapolis: Lerner Publications, 2021.

Muhammad Ali
https://www.ducksters.com/biography/athletes/muhammad_ali.php

National Geographic Kids—The First Olympics
https://kids.nationalgeographic.com/explore/history/first-olympics

Osborne, M. K. *Combat Sports.* Mankato, MN: Amicus, 2020.

Scheff, Matt. *The Summer Olympics: World's Best Athletic Competition.* Minneapolis: Lerner Publications, 2021.

Sports Illustrated Kids—Boxing
https://www.sikids.com/tag/boxing

INDEX

PHOTO ACKNOWLEDGMENTS

Image credits: Ancient Art and Architecture/Alamy Stock Photo, p. 4; Pictorial Press Ltd/Alamy Stock Photo, p. 6; Cris BOURONCLE/Getty Images, p. 7; Focus on Sport/Getty Images, pp. 8, 9 (bottom), 17 (bottom); AP Photo, pp. 9 (top), 13 (all), 18, 23 (top), 25 (bottom), 26, 27 (top); AP Photo/ANTHONY CAMERANO, p. 10; AP Photo/MZ, p. 11 (top); AP Photo/JMH, p. 11 (bottom); Everett Collection Inc/Alamy Stock Photo, p. 12; AP Photo/Isaac Brekken, p. 14; AP Photo/David J. Phillip, p. 15 (top); AP Photo/LM Otero, p. 15 (bottom); Bettmann/Getty Images, p. 16; The Ring Magazine/Getty Images, p. 17 (top); The Stanley Weston Archive/Getty Images, p. 19 (top); PA Images/Alamy Stock Photo, p. 19 (bottom); AP Photo/Alex Menendez, p. 20; AP Photo/Koji Sasahara, p. 21 (top); AP Photo/John Locher, p. 21 (bottom); Chicago History Museum/Alamy Stock Photo, pp. 22, 23 (bottom); PA Images/Alamy Stock Photo, p. 24; Everett Collection Historical/Alamy Stock Photo, p. 25 (top); Focus On Sport/Getty Images, p. 27 (bottom); diy13/Shutterstock.com, p. 28.

Cover: AP Photo/John Locher; Neil Leifer/Getty Images.